HOW DO WE

TIME AND MOTION

JOHN COCKCROFT

GENERAL EDITOR: DAVID PENROSE

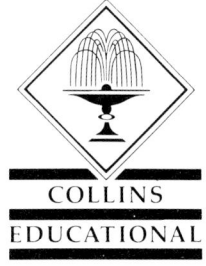

COLLINS EDUCATIONAL

CONTENTS

Transport	3
Travel	7
Turnpikes	10
Canals	19
Railways	26
Ships	35
Bus, tram and trolley	45
Motor cars	51
Transport in photographs	60
Flight	63
Index	64

Transport

Before we think about how people got about in the past, we should be sure we know what 'transport' means.

Classification

People travel from place to place in many different ways. Sometimes it is only people who travel, sometimes they carry cargo or goods. People and cargo need different methods of transport.

Look carefully at this picture. Make a list of the kinds of transport you can see.

Perhaps you can *classify* them into vehicles which carry passengers, and vehicles which carry cargo or goods. Are there any which carry both? Or perhaps you could list them under the headings of land, air or water, according to where they move.

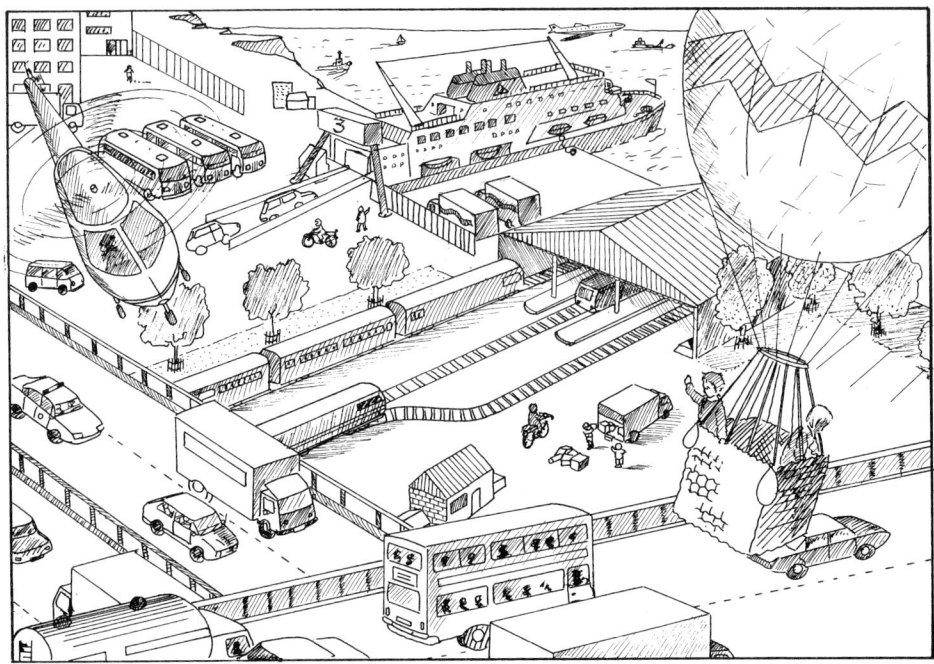

Surveys

As part of his transport project David decided to make a survey of how the children in his class came to school each day. He recorded this information on a pictogram.

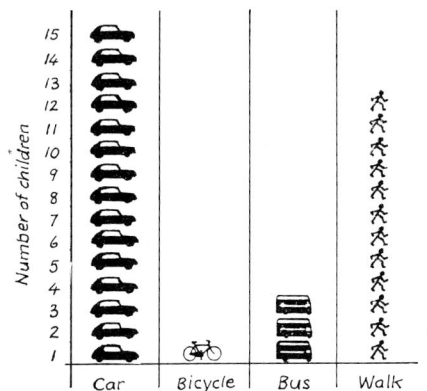

Answer these questions from David's results.
1. Which is the most usual type of transport used?
2. Which is the least usual way of travelling to school?
3. How many pupils are there in David's class?

Now make a pictogram to show how the children in your class travel to school each day.

David had noticed that the High Street near his school was always busy. He thought it might be a good place to do another traffic survey. This is his survey sheet.

	NAME: David Watson	
TRAFFIC SURVEY	DAY: monday	TIME BEGAN: 11.20am
	STREET: High Street	TIME ENDS: 11.30am
CARS	✓✓✓✓✓✓✓✓✓✓✓✓✓✓✓✓✓✓✓✓✓✓✓✓✓✓✓✓✓✓✓✓✓✓✓	
LORRIES	✓✓✓✓ ✓✓✓✓	
BUSES	✓✓✓✓	
MOTOR CYCLES	✓✓✓✓✓	
VANS	✓✓✓✓✓✓✓✓✓✓✓✓✓	
BICYCLES	✓✓	
OTHERS	✓✓	Fire Engine, Police car and caravan

He recorded his findings in a bar-graph.

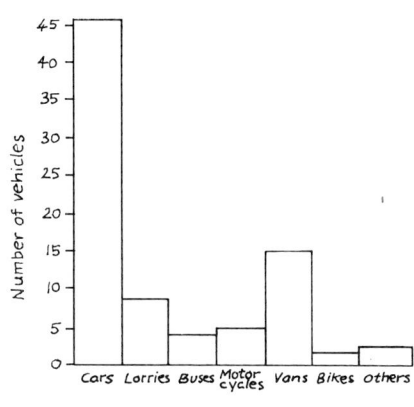

Answer these questions from David's results.
1. On what day was the survey made? At what time?
2. Which was the most common sort of transport?
3. Which was the least common sort of transport he recorded?
4. How many vehicles did David see? Were there any which he wasn't sure how to classify?
5. Do you think that the number and type of vehicles would be the same at this time on every day of the week?
6. When would you expect the High Street to be at its busiest?
7. Look at the plan of David's home town. Would you expect any of the other streets to be busier than the High Street?

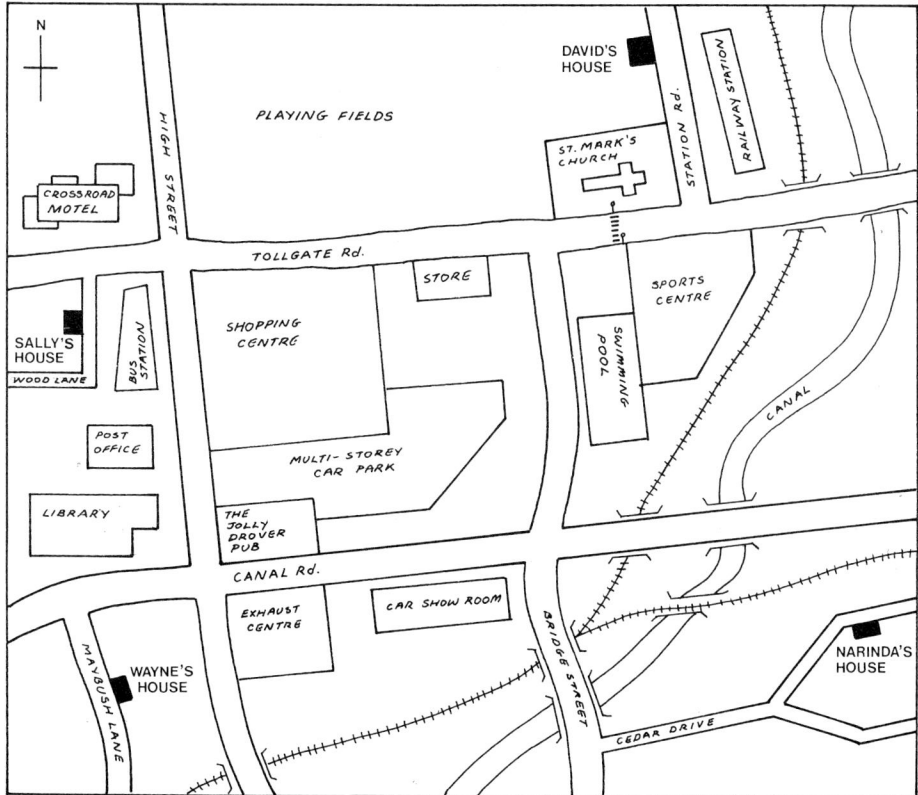

Describing journeys

This is David's description of his route to the swimming pool:

> I leave my house and turn right and walk down Station Road past the railway station on my left and the church on my right. At the church I turn right and walk down Tollgate Road before crossing over to the Sports Centre. I walk through the Sports Centre to the pool.

Now write descriptions like that for the other children mentioned on the map, showing how they would get to the pool on foot.

Look at the map and make a list of anything to do with transport.

Your local area

Use a local plan. Find where the children in your class live, then make a copy of the plan and mark your homes on it.

Choose one of the journeys below and find out from the children in your class what form of transport they would use to make the trip. Make a pictogram or a bar–graph like those on pages 4 and 5.

(a) A journey from home to your local swimming pool or sports centre.

(b) A journey from home to your local shops or town centre.

(c) A journey from home to your local park.
(d) A journey from home to your local library.

Travel

Small journeys

We spend a lot of time moving about. We make many small journeys each day. Each journey is made to satisfy a need. We go from place to place to take things, to collect things or to do something. The things we need are not all to be found in the same place.

Look at this chart. It shows some of the journeys which Joanne made from getting up in the morning until she went to school.

JOURNEY FROM	TO	REASON
Bed	Door	To collect dressing gown
Bedroom	Bathroom	Wash
Bathroom	Bedroom	Dress
Bedroom	Front Door	To collect post
Front Door	Dad in bed	To take letter
Dad in bed	Kitchen refridge	To remove milk
Refrigerator	Table	To put milk out.
Table	Cupboard	To collect cornflakes.
Cupboard	Table	To eat cornflakes.
Table	Hall	To collect schoolbag
Hall	Front door	To go to school.

Make a similar chart and record on it your journeys for the same time of day.

Draw a plan of part of your home and mark on it the journeys from your chart like the one done here for Joanne. Notice that some places are very busy; other places are hardly used at all at this time of day.

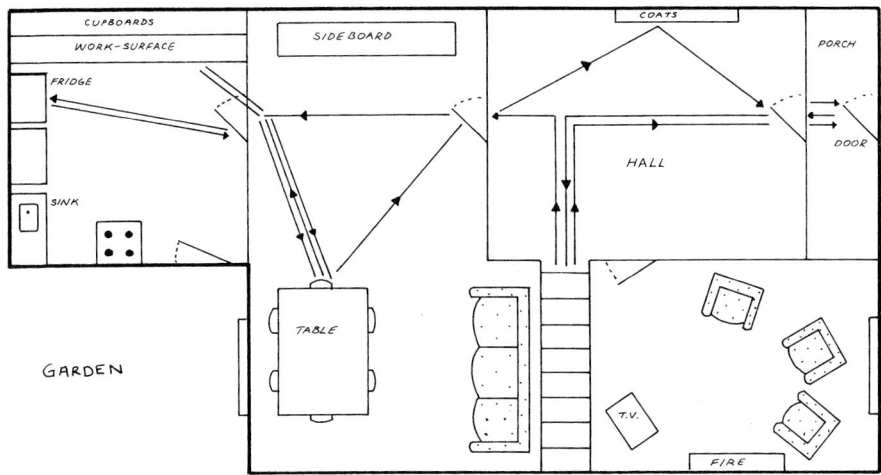

You could record your class's journeys around your school in the same way. First try to decide which are the busiest places. Does your journeys map show that you were right? Perhaps you can make up suitable traffic signs for these busy places.

Kinds of transport

Everywhere people are on the move. Some are just moving themselves from place to place; others have jobs where they spend their time moving people or goods. Can you think of any?

The type of transport which people use depends on where and how far they want to go, what they want to carry, how fast they need to travel and how much the journey will cost.

Here are loads to be carried and their transport. Match each type of transport with its load.

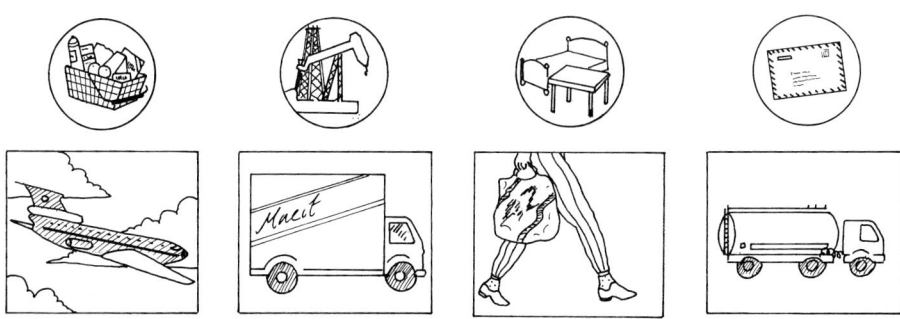

Day and night, cargoes are being transported all round the country and all over the world. To move a single cargo many different forms of transport are often used. Look at these pictures and make a list of all the types of transport which might be used to get each product to a place where someone can use it.

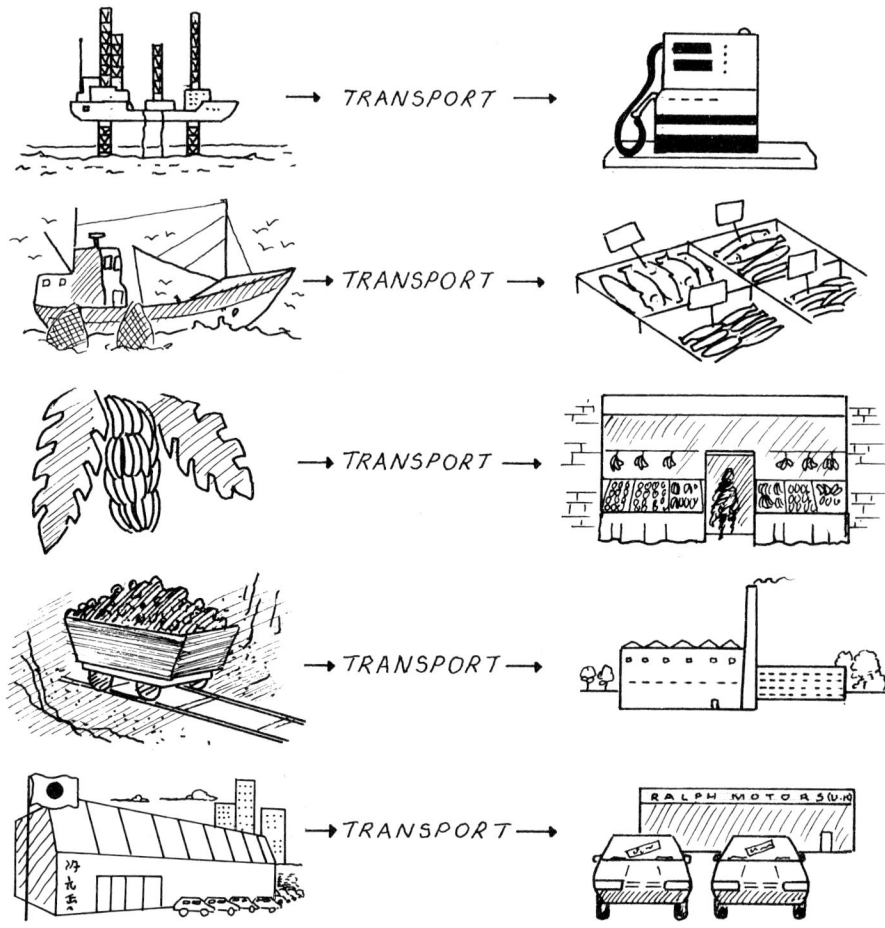

If you had to make the following journeys, what type of transport would you use?

1 km to collect the shopping.
10 km to the railway station to collect a suitcase.
100 km to take a relative a birthday cake.
1000 km to deliver furniture from a factory.
10 000 km to spend a holiday in Australia.

Turnpikes

For centuries Britain's roads seemed to be nobody's business. The Romans built a fine road *network* about 2000 years ago, but they left after about 400 years and the roads were no longer looked after. As Britain grew more prosperous, more people and goods needed to travel and roads had to be improved.

During the eighteenth century (more than 250 years ago), groups of people, often landowners, set up in business to build and look after roads. They collected fees or *tolls* from travellers and spent the money on the roads. They called the roads *turnpikes* and their business companies — which they hoped to run at a profit — *turnpike trusts*.

You may have travelled on a modern road where you had to pay a toll, or perhaps you have paid to drive through the Dartford Tunnel under the River Thames, or to cross the bridge over the River Forth.

If a group of people wanted to set up a turnpike trust, they had to arrange for Parliament to pass an act to allow them to do it. There were many of these acts during the eighteenth century and the first part of the nineteenth, before railways began to spread. You can see part of a turnpike act on page 11.

Records of turnpikes

There may have been a turnpike road near where you live. Because money had to be collected and spent, a turnpike road was a business which had to be well managed. All decisions made by the management had to be recorded and details of the money collected and spent noted down. A lot of these records have been kept and can be found in your local records office or archives department.

Looking at the documents

This is the introduction, or *preamble*, to a turnpike act.

1. What do you think the road between Ipswich and Stratford St Mary was like in about the year 1810?
2. What does 'incommodious' mean?
3. When was a decision made to improve the road?

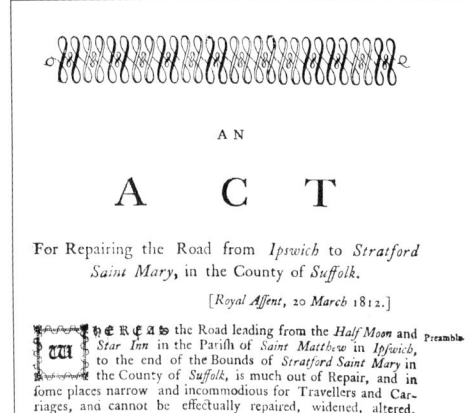

These records, made in January and June 1830, are of a surveyor's daily expenditure on repairing the roads. At this time roads were usually made of stones. These had to be broken up to the right size and carefully laid down so that the smallest and finest were on the surface. This was done by hand. If a lot of traffic was using the road, or if the weather was very bad, repairs were often necessary.

1. Try and find some of the jobs which had to be done.
2. Why do you think the road had to be 'scraped'?
3. In what ways did the weather make work for the road-workers?

11

This is the record of a meeting of a turnpike trust.
1. When and where was the meeting held?
2. Find the paragraph beginning 'Mr Sinnott attended the meeting . . .' What problem does it show? You may need to look up the word 'evading'.
3. What did the meeting decide to do about this problem? Do the people who were there seem to be in a great hurry to get something done? How long will it be before the next meeting?

At a General Meeting of the Trustees appointed by virtue of an Act of Parliament passed in the second year of the reign of His Majesty King William the Fourth entitled "An Act for more effectually repairing the road from Ipswich to Stratford Saint Mary in the country of Suffolk" holden pursuant to notice at the White Elm Inn at Copdock on Friday the twenty-fifth day of July, one thousand eight hundred and forty-five due notice hereof having been first given.

Present

    John Gosnall Esq in the Chair
    James Josselyn
    N H Whisnper
    John Josselyn
    William Back

It is ordered that five pounds ten shillings for a year's expense of lighting the gate up to the twenty-fifth day of March one thousand eight hundred and forty-five be paid to Mr Sinnott.

Mr Sinnott attended the meeting and requested the Trustees to erect a side bar at Copdock Pound to prevent many persons from evading the payment of tolls.

It was resolved that the clerk do call a special meeting for the purpose of consulting about the propriety of erecting a side bar or side bars to prevent such evasion of tolls. Such meeting to be held at the White Elm Inn at Copdock on Friday the fifteenth day of August next at twelve o'clock at noon.

It is ordered that Mr Archer's bill for stone for the new toll house amounting to thirteen shillings and sixpence be paid by the surveyor.

Stage and mail coaches

Stage coach companies ran regular services along the turnpike roads. The horses had to be changed about every 10 or 12 miles because that was about as far as they could go without tiring too much. These distances were called 'stages'. The horses were kept at inns along the road. Coachmen were proud of leaving and arriving on time. (Can you think where the word 'slowcoach' comes from?)

A print of a busy coaching scene outside a hotel in the late eighteenth century

The post was carried in special mail coaches which also took passengers. They were light and fast and had an armed guard in case of highwaymen. As you can see from this poster, the guard was not always good enough.

£1000 Reward.

STOLEN

FROM THE IPSWICH MAIL,
On its way from London, *on the Night of the 11th Sept. Inst.* the following
COUNTRY BANK NOTES:
Ipswich Bank, 5, & 10*l.* Notes.
ALEXANDERS & Co. on HOARE & Co.

Woodbridge Bank, 1, 5, & 10*l.* Notes.
ALEXANDERS & Co. on FRYS & Co.

Manningtree Bank, 1, 5, & 10*l.* Notes.
ALEXANDER & Co. on FRYS & Co.

Hadleigh Bank, 1, 5, & 10*l.* Notes.
ALEXANDER & Co. on FRYS & Co.
Particulars of which will be furnished at the different Bankers.

Whoever will give Information, either at ALEXANDERS and Co. or at FRYS and Co., St Mildred's Court, Poultry, so that the Parties may be apprehended, shall on his or their Conviction, and the Recovery of the Property, receive the above REWARD.

Coaching inns

Travel on turnpike roads was slow by our standards, but quick for the time. If a journey took more than one day some travellers would stop at a coaching inn rather than continue their journey through the night.

Here is a picture of a famous London coaching inn, The Swan With Two Necks, together with a coach timetable.

1. How can you tell that the coaches in the courtyard are Royal Mail coaches? Look at the door of the coach just leaving the inn.
2. What do you think the ground floor rooms round the yard were used for? What about the upper rooms?
3. What sort of jobs can you see being done?
4. If you wanted to take the first post coach to Edinburgh what time would you leave the inn?
5. Supposing you missed the first coach, what time was the next Edinburgh coach?

You could go to France from The Swan With Two Necks. Find the entries on the timetable which show this. Are any other foreign places mentioned?

Find the entry on the timetables which shows the place nearest to where you live. Work out when you would have to leave London to get there by coach. If you live in London, when would you have to leave to get to Liverpool or Bristol in order to board a ship for America? This is the sort of thing which a London businessman of the time might have done. There were no aeroplanes then.

14

THE
PUBLIC CONVEYANCES
FROM THE
Swan with 2 Necks
ROYAL MAIL OFFICE,
Are constructed upon the most approved principles of Safety.

SHOULD ANY
IRREGULARITIES OCCUR
IT IS REQUESTED THAT
IMMEDIATE APPLICATION
BE MADE TO
W. CHAPLIN & Co.

SWAN WITH TWO NECKS, LAD LANE,
GENERAL COACH OFFICE.

The following ROYAL MAILS

Leave the above Office every Evening at a Quarter-past Seven; on Sundays at Seven o'Clock.

BATH and EXETER ROYAL MAIL, through Devizes, Melksham, Wells, Bridgewater, Taunton, and Collumpton.
BIRMINGHAM ROYAL MAIL, through Stony Stratford, Daventry, and Coventry.
BRISTOL ROYAL MAIL, through Reading, Newbury, Malboro', Calne, and Chippenham.
CAMBRIDGE ROYAL MAIL, through Buntingford, Royston, and Melbourne.
CARLISLE and EDINBURGH ROYAL MAIL, through Chorley, Preston, and Garstang.
CHESTER ROYAL MAIL, through Salop, Ellesmere, & Wrexham.
DEVONPORT ROYAL MAIL, through Chudleigh and Ashburton.
EXETER ROYAL MAIL, through Salisbury, Sherborne, Yeovil, Crewkerne, and Honiton.
HOLYHEAD ROYAL MAIL, through Stony Stratford, Towcester, Daventry, Dunchurch, Coventry, Birmingham, Wolverhampton, Shiffnall, Shrewsbury, Oswestry, Langollen, Corwen, and Bangor.
HULL and LINCOLN ROYAL MAIL, through Peterborough and Sleaford.
KIDDERMINSTER ROYAL MAIL, through Birmingham, Dudley, and Stourbridge.
LIVERPOOL ROYAL MAIL, through Dunchurch, Coleshill, Lichfield, Newcastle, and Warrington.
LYNN and WELLS ROYAL MAIL, through Ely and Downham.
MANCHESTER ROYAL MAIL, thro' Northampton, Harborough, Leicester, Derby, Ashbourn, Leek, and Macclesfield.
MILFORD HAVEN ROYAL MAIL, through Cardiff, Swansea, Carmarthen, and Haverfordwest.
NORTH DEVON and BARNSTAPLE MAIL, through Bampton, and South Molton.
NORWICH ROYAL MAIL, through Chelmsford, Colchester, and Ipswich.
PLYMOUTH and FALMOUTH ROYAL MAIL.
STROUD ROYAL MAIL, thro' Abingdon, Farringdon, Cirencester, and Chalford.
SOUTHAMPTON and POOLE ROYAL MAIL, through Farnham, Alton, Alresford, and Winchester.
SCARBORO' ROYAL MAIL, thro' Beverly, Driffield & Bridlington.

POST COACHES.

MORNING
	Time.
ABERYSTWITH, through Leominster	quarter before 8
BIRMINGHAM, (Tantivy) through Oxford	7
BIRMINGHAM, (Tally Ho!) in 11 hours, thro' Stony Stratford	8
BLANDFORD, (Herald) thro' Basingstoke & Salisbury, half-past	8
BRISTOL and BATH, (Emerald) without Fees, through Devizes and Melksham	7
BRISTOL and BATH, (Cooper's) Old Company's Coach, through Calne and Chippenham, without Fees to Coachman and Guard	7
BRIGHTON, through Reigate	8
BRIGHTON, through Hixstead	8
CANTERBURY, through Faversham	10
CANTERBURY	quarter before 8
CARMARTHEN, through Abergavenny	quarter before 8
CHELTENHAM, (Retaliator) thro' Wycombe & Oxford, quart. bef.	8
CHESTER, through Birmingham	8
COVENTRY	8
DARLINGTON, (Highflyer) through York	quarter before 9
DEAL, through Sandwich	8
DERBY, (Times) through Loughborough	quarter before 7
DONCASTER, (Highflyer) thro' Stamford & Grantham, quart, bef.	8
DORCHESTER, (Herald) thro' Sutton Scotney & Salisbury half-p.	8
DOVOR	quarter before 8 and quarter before 10
DUDLEY	quarter before 8
DURHAM, (Highflyer) thro' Retford & Ferrybridge quarter before	9
EDINBURGH, through York	quarter before 9
EXETER, (Herald) through Salisbury, and Dorchester half-past	8
FALMOUTH, (Herald) only one Night out, through Launceston, Bodmin, and Truro	half-past 8
GLOUCESTER, (Retaliator) through Northleach	quarter before 8
HOLYHEAD, (Tally Ho!) through Shrewsbury	8
LEAMINGTON	quarter before 8
LEICESTER, (Times) through Harboro'	quarter before 8
LEICESTER, (Red Rover) thro' Northampton & Welford, ½ past	10
LIVERPOOL, (Tally Ho!) through Birmingham	8
LIVERPOOL, (Red Rover) through Welford, Ashby-de-la-Zouch, Uttoxeter, Burslem, and Hanley	half-past 10
MANCHESTER, (Tally Ho!) thro' Birmingham, with preference to sleep at Birmingham, or proceed at pleasure	8
MARGATE, through Canterbury	quarter before 8
NEWBURY, (Zephyr) through Wokingham, and Aldermaston	10
NEWCASTLE, (Highflyer) through Thirsk, Northallerton, and Rushiford	quarter before 8
NORWICH, (Times) through Bury and Scole	half-past 5
NOTTINGHAM, (Times) through Northampton	quarter before 7
OXFORD, through High Wycomb	quarter before 8
OXFORD, (Royal William) through Uxbridge	12
PARIS, by way of Dovor	quarter before 8
PARIS, by way of Dovor	quarter before 10
PLYMOUTH, (Herald) thro' Blandford and Honiton	half-past 8
PORTSMOUTH, through Godalming	8
RAMSGATE, through Rochester	8
READING, (Zephyr) through Windsor and Bracknell	10
SALISBURY, through Basingstoke and Stockbridge	half-past 8
STAMFORD, (Highflyer) thro' Baldock & Wansford, half-past	9
SOUTHAMPTON and LYMINGTON (Independent)	quarter-past 7
WORCESTER, through Tewksbury	quarter before 8
WARWICK, through Coventry	8
WEYMOUTH, (Herald) thro' Salisbury & Dorchester	half-past 8

MORNING CONTINUED
	Time.
WINDSOR and ETON	quarter before 8
YORK, (Highflyer) through Newark & Doncaster, quarter before	9

AFTERNOON
BRIGHTON	3
BRIGHTON	4
BATH, (Age) through Newbury and Melksham	half-past 3
BIRMINGHAM, (Greyhound) thro' Stony Stratford in 11 hours	half-past 6
BIRMINGHAM, (Erin-go-Bragh) through Woodstock	half-past 6
BRISTOL, (Age) through Marlborough and Devizes	half-past 3
BRISTOL and BATH, (Cooper's) Old Company's Coach, through Devizes and Melksham	5
CAMBRIDGE, (Rocket) thro' Ware, Buntingford, and Royston	2
CANTERBURY, (Tally Ho!) through Ospringe	half-past 2
CANTERBURY	7
CARLISLE, (Defiance) through Preston	half-past 6
CARLISLE, (Royal Bruce) through Garstang	quarter before 8
CHESTER, (Greyhound) through Birmingham	half-past 6
COVENTRY, (Greyhound) through Dunstable	half-past 6
DERBY, (Defiance) through Leicester	half-past 6
DERBY, (Royal Bruce) through Northampton	quarter before 8
DOVOR	7
DUDLEY, (Greyhound) through Coventry	half-past 6
EDINBURGH, (Defiance) through Carlisle	half-past 6
EDINBURGH, (Bruce) through Carlisle	quarter before 8
GLASGOW, (Defiance) thro' Kendal and Dumfries	half-past 6
GLASGOW, (Bruce) thro' Kendal and Dumfries	half-past 8
HOLYHEAD, (Greyhound) through Shrewsbury	half-past 6
IPSWICH, through Colchester	quarter before 8
LEAMINGTON	quarter before 5
LEICESTER, (Defiance) through Northampton	half-past 6
LEICESTER, (Bruce) through Harborough	quarter before 8
LIVERPOOL, (Tartar) thro' Leamington & Warwick quart. before	5
MANCHESTER, (Defiance) thro' Leek &, Macclesfield, half-past	6
MANCHESTER, (Bruce) through Derby, Belper, Matlock, Bakewell, and Buxton	quarter before 8
MILFORD HAVEN, (Age) through Swansea	half-past 3
NOTTINGHAM, (Commercial) through Northampton and Leicester	quarter before 5
NOTTINGHAM, (Defiance) through Leicester	half-past 6
NOTTINGHAM, (Bruce) through Loughborough, quarter before	8
OXFORD, through Henly	half-past 3
PARIS, through Amiens and Chantilly	7
PORTSMOUTH, through Godalming and Guildford	6
PORTSMOUTH, through Petersfield	half-past 7
SHREWSBURY, (Greyhound) thro' Birmingham	half-past 6
SOUTHAMPTON, (Royal William) through Farnham, Alton, Alresford, and Winchester	6
SOUTHAMPTON, (Quicksilver) through Basingstoke and Winchester	quarter past 8
STAFFORD, through Wolverhampton and Penkridge, half-past	6
SWANSEA, through Bristol and Cardiff	half-past 3 and 5
TAUNTON, through Cross and Bridgewater	half-past 3 and 5
TENBY, through Newport and Carmarthen	half-past 3 and 5
WARWICK, (Tartar) through Southam	quarter before 5
WINDSOR and ETON	4

Parcels and Luggage conveyed Daily to all parts of the North, and to every City and Manufacturing Town in the Kingdom.
The Public are respectfully informed, that every information relative to the Steam Packets connected with the above Coaches, may be obtained at the Swan with Two Necks; Spread Eagle, Gracechurch Street; and Spread Eagle Office, Regent Circus, Piccadilly.

Passengers and Parcels are regularly booked at the Spread Eagle Office, Regent Circus, Piccadilly, and Angel Inn, St. Clement's Strand, and conveyed by all the above Coaches. Goods received for the Monarch, James Watt, and Soho Steam Packets, for Edinbro', Glasgow, Paisley, & all Parts of Scotland, every Saturday till 6 o'Clock.—WILLIAM CHAPLIN & Co.

The Great White Horse

If you have read *The Census* in this series, you will know about the Great White Horse in Ipswich. It was a coaching inn and the famous writer Charles Dickens stayed there. He wrote about it in one of his books, *Pickwick Papers*. This was published during 1836 and 1837 so we know Dickens must have been there before then.

Try reading Dickens's description of the inn. It is rather difficult and you may need a dictionary. Your teacher will help you.

> In the main street of Ipswich . . . stands an inn known far and wide by the appellation of the Great White Horse, rendered the more conspicuous by a stone statue of some rampacious animal with flowing mane and tail, distantly resembling an insane cart-horse, which is elevated above the principal door. The Great White Horse is famous in the neighbourhood, in the same degree as a prize ox, or county paper-chronicled turnip, or unwieldy pig — for its enormous size. Never were such labyrinths of uncarpeted passages, such clusters of mouldy, ill-lighted rooms, such huge numbers of small dens for eating or sleeping in, beneath any one roof as are collected together between the four walls of the Great White Horse at Ipswich.
>
> It was at the door of this overgrown tavern that the London coach stopped, at the same hour every evening; and it was from this same London coach, that Mr Pickwick, Sam Weller, and Mr Peter Magnus dismounted, on the particular evening to which this chapter of our history bears reference.

Do you think Dickens liked The Great White Horse? *Pickwick Papers* is a story, so perhaps all these details are not quite true. The owner of The Great White Horse may have read *Pickwick Papers*, as it was a very popular book. Would he have been pleased with the description?

Tollgates

Here is a board showing the amounts or tolls you had to pay to use a turnpike. For coach travellers the tolls were quite expensive. Poor people hardly ever thought of going in a coach, though they might walk along a turnpike as shepherds with a flock of sheep, or as cowmen with a herd of cows.

Look back at the record of the meeting on page 12. Find the paragraph which mentions lighting. Obviously this was an important matter which had to be recorded. Why do you think it was important to light tollgates?

The coming of railways

When the railways arrived, (see p. 26), it was not long before people saw that trains had advantages over stagecoaches. Make a list of advantages and disadvantages.

What did the Ipswich coach companies do when the railway reached as far as Colchester? Look at this advertisement from 1844. How long did it take a traveller to reach London from Ipswich using coaches and the train?

COACHES.

From the Great White Horse Hotel, the White Hart, and the Suffolk Hotel.

Mails to London, at ½-past 11 night, and to Norwich and Yarmouth, at ½ past 3 morning

From the Suffolk Hotel.

The Original Blue, to *London*, at ¼ past 1 afternoon, and to Yarmouth, at ½ past 1 aft. daily, except Sund

To Bury St Edmunds & Cambridge, at 11 morning and 4 afternoon, daily, except Sunday, through Needham-market and Stowmarket

From Haxell's office, Brook street.

To meet the *Eastern Counties' Railway Trains* at *Colchester*, the QUICKSILVER, at 7 morning; the RETALIATOR (from Woodbridge) at 20 min. before 9 morning; the SHANNON (from Halesworth) at ½ past 11 mg; and the NORWICH DAY COACH, at ½ past one, daily, except Sunday. By these conveyances, passengers go from *Ipswich to London* in 4½ hours; and persons going by the Quicksilver, and returning the same day, have five hours in London

Soon the railways took over from the coaches and were able to offer special cheap fares, as you can see from this advertisement from a newspaper published in 1860. Ordinary people could afford to travel more. Before the railway few people in Ipswich would ever have thought of going to London. The day of the turnpikes was over.

What result arising from the coming of the railways is this cartoon from the mid-nineteenth century showing?

Canals

Leeds-Liverpool Canal

In the days before railways it was difficult to move heavy goods. Roads were often not good enough.

Where there were rivers boats were used. Rivers were improved by making them deeper or by straightening and widening them. Gradually people thought of making canals, either to join rivers or to make new *waterways*.

The longest canal in Great Britain is the Leeds and Liverpool Canal.

You can see from this map that it joins up with the River Aire, so that there is a waterway right across the country from one sea to the other.

What advantages were there in linking the east and west coasts of Great Britain?

This is how the advantages of this canal were described in a directory in 1792. The language is difficult to understand so it has been rewritten into modern English on the following page.

> Besides the saving in the enormous expence of land-carriage, the whole country through which the canal passes is supplied with wool, corn, hides, tallow, &c. from Ireland, with the produce of America and whatever else is imported at Liverpool. The same countries can also obtain linen, tin-plate, timber, iron, hemp, flax, Russian linen, pot-ash, and all the eastern commodities brought to the port of Hull; and in like manner all the exports are benefited and encouraged. Without the advantage of this internal navigation from east to west, vessels would be obliged to go many leagues round the island to establish an intercourse between our manufactures, unless the merchants chose to submit to the heavy imposts of land conveyance.
>
> UNIVERSAL BRITISH DIRECTORY 1792

As well as saving money on land transport the areas round the canal are supplied with wood, corn, animal skins, tallow etc from Ireland and also all the goods from America which arrive in Britain at the port of Liverpool. The areas round the canal are also supplied with linen, tin-plate, timber, iron, hemp, flax, Russian linen, pot-ash and all the goods which arrive from eastern countries at the port of Hull. These areas can also export their goods to either Liverpool or Hull easily. If there was no canal, ships carrying all these goods would have to go many leagues round Britain to set up trade with the east and west coasts, unless the merchants decided to use land transport which is very expensive.

Trace the map of England on page 19 and show how goods might have gone by sea between Liverpool and Hull if there had been no canal.

There had to be an Act of Parliament to make the canal because the building of one would affect so many people. Can you think of any who would be affected?

Between Leeds and Liverpool are the Pennine Hills. Canals cannot go directly up or downhill, so *locks*, tunnels and *aqueducts* have to be built.

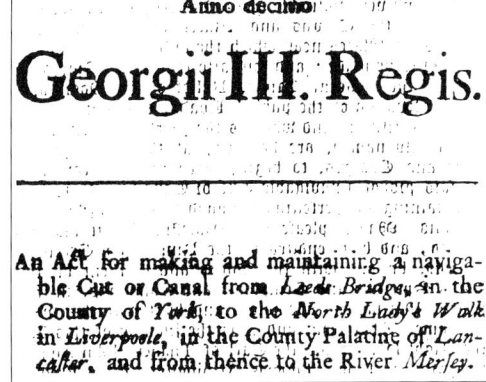

An eighteenth century print showing the Burton Aqueduct

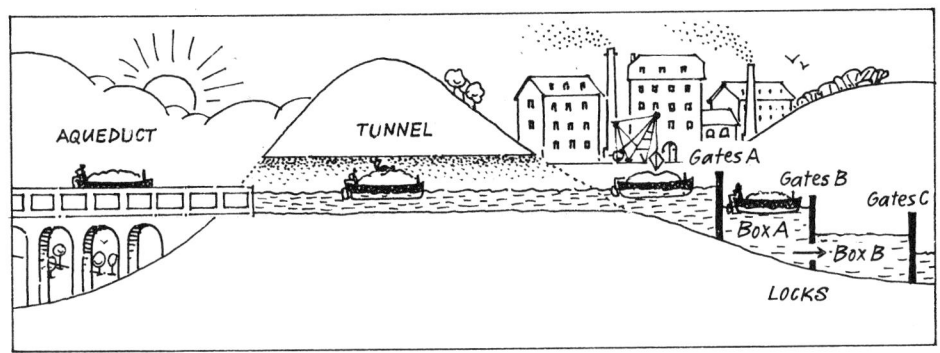

Locks are either a single or a series of boxes with gates. Moving downhill, the barge floats into box A, gates A, B & C close and water flows into box B through *sluices* until the water level in both boxes is the same. Gates B are opened and the barge floats through into box B. Can you work out how the barge can move uphill from box B to box A?

The canals, locks, tunnels and aqueducts were built by *navigators* or *navvies*. Notice that a canal was also called a *navigation*.
Look this word up in a dictionary.

The navvies did not have mechanical diggers or bulldozers to help them. These had not been invented. All they had were picks, shovels, wheelbarrows and sometimes horses. Later on railways were also built by navvies. Look at the picture on page 33.

This is what the Bingley Five Rise locks looked like in 1906 and in 1986. What differences can you see? Why do you think the locks are called Bingley Five Rise?

Here is a newspaper report about the opening of the locks at Bingley.

> We hear from Bingley that 20 miles of the Grand Canal between Liverpool and Leeds was opened yesterday for business, from Skipton to below the junction with the Bradford Canal, in the presence of several thousand spectators. From Bingley to about three miles downwards, the noblest works of the kind that perhaps are to be found in the same extent in the universe are exhibited. A fivefold, a threefold, a twofold, and a single lock, making a fall of 120 feet; a large aqueduct bridge of seven arches over the River Aire, and an aqueduct and a large banking over the Shipley Valley. Five boats . . . passed the grand lock, the first of which descended through a fall of sixty feet in less than twenty-nine minutes, to the amazement and delight of the spectators. These works (in the opinions of the best judges) are executed in a masterly manner, and the locks and their machinery excellent. This joyful . . . event was welcomed with the ringing of Bingley Bells, a band of music, the firing of guns by the neighbouring Militia (Soldiers), the shouts of the spectators . . .
>
> LEEDS INTELLIGENCER, 22 March 1774

How many years ago was this? What other canal structures were opened at the same time? How can you tell from this report that people were impressed by the locks when they were opened? How many feet could the boats go down by using the locks?

Canals were used to transport goods to and from factories. They were built during the *Industrial Revolution* when factories became bigger and used steam engines. Why should it be useful for a manufacturer to build his factory next to a canal?

Travellers using the canals had to pay tolls as they did on the turnpike roads. There were toll offices situated at various points along the canals.

The photograph on page 23 was taken from the air. It shows Saltaire, a factory village near Bingley, on the Leeds and Liverpool canal. The railway had been built by this time. Look at the transport routes in the photograph. Why is the factory well-placed?

Compare the photograph with the plan. What differences are there between them? Which do you think was made first, the plan or the photograph?

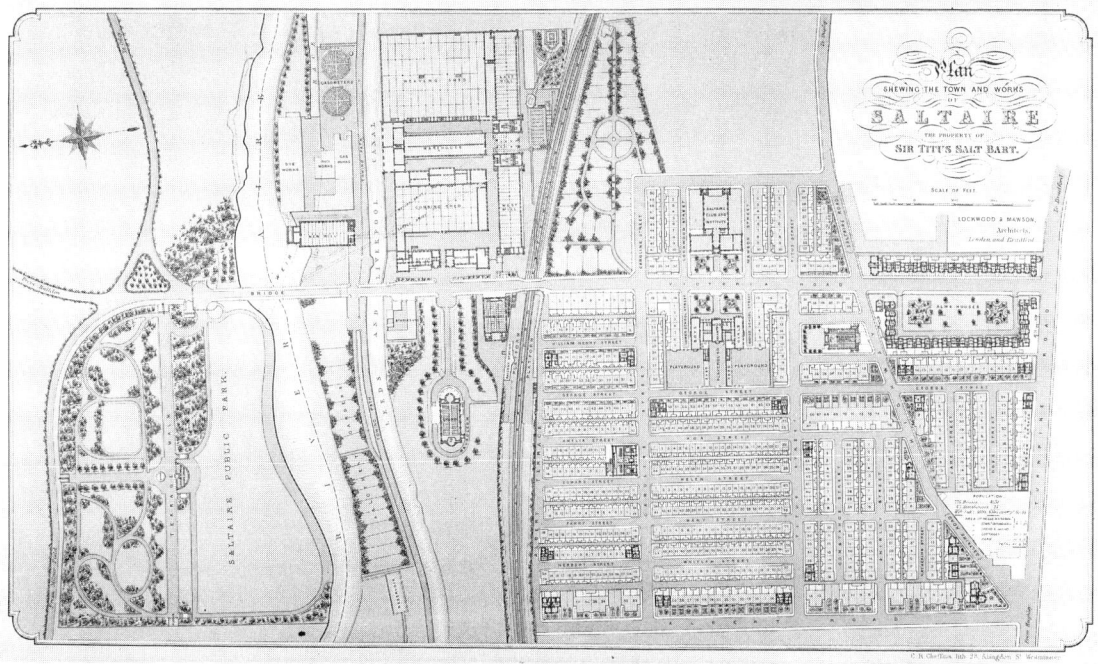

There are stables shown near the canal on the plan. Why do you think stables were needed? If you can't guess, look at photograph A on page 25 for a clue. Have you ever walked along a towpath by a canal? What was it originally used for?

One of these pictures shows 'raw material arriving by canal'. Where do you think this piece of evidence actually comes from. Try looking at the acknowledgements on the inside back page. What sort of cargoes might barges have brought to this factory? What might they have carried away?

Compare the photograph with this one, taken recently. What do you think has happened to the canal now?

24

Here are three pictures of barges on the canal taken at different times. How have barges changed in their use?

A *Horse boat with family crew, about 1900*

B *Goods-carrying barge in the early 1900s*

C *A modern-day pleasure barge*

What form of power does each barge use to make it move?

Where did the bargees shown in picture A live?

Imagine you and your family live on this barge. What problems would you have? For example, think about shopping, cooking, washing, the weather.

The coming of the railways meant the end of canals as an important means of transport in the same way as it led to the decline of coaching and turnpikes.

25

Railways

Museums

One way of finding out about history is to visit the past. You don't need a time machine to be a time traveller, just visit a museum. There are many different kinds. In this section we shall be looking at museums connected with railway history. Perhaps there is a railway museum or a 'preserved railway' near you. Are there other museums near where you live?

Railway tracks

Railways began long before steam engines or electric locomotives were ever thought of. Most roads were very poor and in bad weather wagons sank into the mud. If you have tried pushing a heavy wheelbarrow over a muddy garden you will know what happens. People working on a building site have the same problem. To make their job easier they build their own kind of railway.

The first rail tracks were made of wood. They were called wagonways because they were used to move wagons which were laden with coal or other heavy things and pulled by horses. What would happen to wooden rails which continually had heavy wagons moving over them? Later on, rail builders laid metal plates over the wooden rails so that they did not wear out so quickly. In time the whole rail came to be made of metal.

Look at the picture at the top of page 27. What is in the wagon? What will the horse be used for? What can you see in the background which suggests that the load has a long way to travel? If you look carefully you can see that the wheels of the wagon cannot possibly run along the rails without some kind of support. Keeping the wheels on the track was a common problem.

Solutions to problems

There are two ways of stopping the wheels falling off the track. You can a) use wheels which have a *flange*, (a projecting rim), or b) you can have a track with a flange, called a *plateway*. Look at these photographs of old railways and decide which solution to the problem each one shows. What do modern train wheels look like?

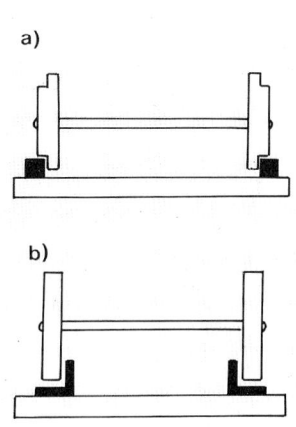

Rails must be firmly fixed to the ground. Can you tell how this was done from these pictures? What about modern railway tracks?

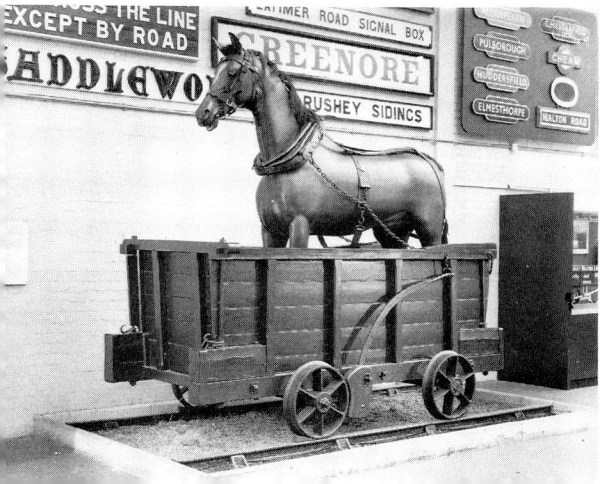

Public railways

At first, railways were built by private businesses for their own use — by mining companies to move coal, for example.

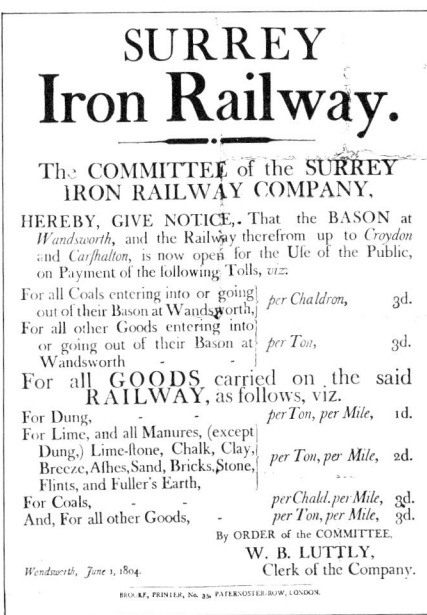

The first public railway in the world was the Surrey Iron Railway, which opened in 1803. Here is one of its advertisements. You can see that people had to pay a toll to use the railway, just as they had to pay a toll to use turnpikes and canals.

What sort of goods were carried on the railway? Do you think that this railway carried ordinary passengers?

What does 'chaldron' mean?

Use the Acknowledgements at the back of this book to discover where the pictures in this section come from. You can buy some of them at museum shops like the one at the National Railway Museum at York.

The Stockton and Darlington Railway

At the beginning of the nineteenth century, almost 200 years ago, many factories used coal to run their machines. But coal is very heavy and factories needed large amounts. In south Durham coal was carried from the mines by road to the docks at Stockton, but this was expensive. The mine-owners wanted to build a canal between the mines around Darlington and Stockton but the land was too hilly for a canal. They decided to build a *plateway* so that coal could be put straight into the trucks at the mines and taken straight to the docks.

They asked George Stephenson to build the plateway for them, but he was a maker of locomotives and he persuaded them to build a railway which could use steam locomotives instead of horses.

Look at the share certificate of the company. What do the picture and seal tell you about how the owners intended the railway to be used?

29

This picture shows the opening, in 1825, of the Stockton and Darlington Railway, with George Stephenson driving his new engine called Locomotion.

Look at the picture carefully. What do you think the horseman is doing in front of the train?

The Stockton and Darlington Railway Company was set up like a canal or turnpike trust. Its main purpose was simply to provide a road which others might use with their own vehicles for a payment. At first the single-line track was shared by steam locomotives, horse wagons and a rail stagecoach. Can you think of any problems this might have caused?

What people thought

Not everybody liked the idea of steam travel. Steam trains went much faster than the horse-drawn coaches and carts everybody was used to. Speeds such as 18 or 20 miles an hour were thought to be dreadfully dangerous. People protested against railways. Can you think of arguments which they might have used to get the railways stopped? What do you think the owners of canals and coach businesses thought about it?

This is how the Locomotion might have looked when it worked on the Stockton and Darlington Railway. This copy or *replica* can be seen at Beamish Open Air Museum in Northumberland.

The wagons do not seem very satisfactory for passengers. What would they be better used for?

Look at the engine-driver. Do you think he was in danger? What would it have been like on a cold, wet morning in January?

The Liverpool and Manchester Railway

While he was building the Stockton and Darlingon railway George Stephenson was visited by businessmen from Liverpool and Manchester. They wanted him to build a railway between the two towns, (see the map on page 29). This railway was opened in 1830.

George's son, Robert, won a competition to see who could build the best locomotive for the new railway. His was called the Rocket. You can see the Rocket in the Science Museum in London together with a replica of it.

How does the original differ from the replica?

Coaches

Why is a railway carriage called a coach? Perhaps these pictures from the National Railway Museum in York might give you a clue. Write a description of each one, noting differences to do with comfort, space, luggage and warmth.

Navvies

The early railways were built by navvies. If you can't remember where this name comes from, look back at page 21. This model of one is in the National Railway Museum in York.

There were very few machines to help the navvies in the early days of railway building. They often had only picks and shovels and their own strength.

Building a railway line

Railways have to be built on even ground as far as possible. Ordinary trains cannot travel on rails up or down steep slopes because the wheels slip.

Rising ground has to be avoided or cut through either as a tunnel or a cutting. Falling ground has to be crossed by a railway bridge, called a *viaduct*, or an embankment. Engineers tried to lay out a line so that the earth from a cutting could be used for an embankment. This was known as 'cut and fill'.

In this picture, drawn in 1839, navvies are building a cutting using 'barrow runs'. Look carefully and see if you can work out how a barrow run works.

Make a copy of this diagram. Mark on your diagram where the engineer would build a cutting, a tunnel, a viaduct and an embankment in order to build a railway to the town.

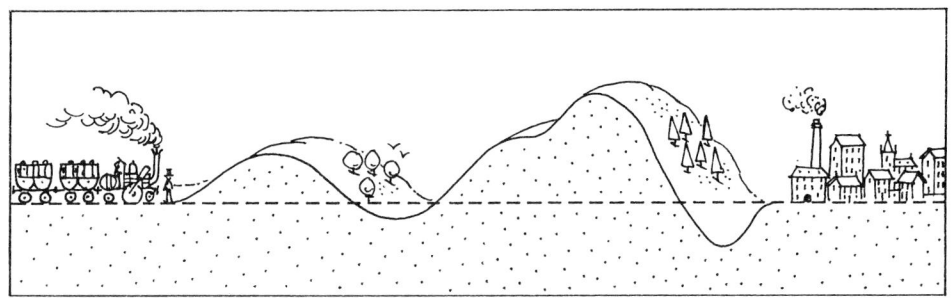

Railway companies

After 1830 passenger railways developed quickly and many different railway companies were founded. Gradually they joined together and by 1923 there were only four: London, Midland & Scottish; London & North Eastern; Great Western; and Southern. Their names or initials can be seen on the sides of locomotives in museums. Which companies do the examples below belong to? Find out which areas the companies served. Besides the actual names, your parents or grandparents may be able to help you. After the second World War, in 1948, all the railways were *nationalised* so that there was just one railway company owned and controlled by the Government. What is this company called? Do you know what the common logo looks like that is on all the trains?

Ships

Boats are probably as old as our desire to travel. Nobody knows when the first boat was invented. Perhaps it was the result of someone's need to take a short-cut across a river, rather than walk a long way upstream until the river could be crossed on foot. Perhaps someone chose to cross a lake rather than walk all the way round. Perhaps someone just wanted to see what the land was like on the other side of the water.

We can find out about early boats

> by looking at the remains of those that have been found,
> by looking at very old pictures,
> by seeing how people build simple boats today,
> or by looking at boats which are built by very old methods.

For example, the coracle was in use at least 2000 years ago, at the time of Julius Caesar. People still make them today.

Roman ships

There are no Roman ships like Julius Caesar's left, but we do have clues as to what they looked like. This sculpture shows a Roman trading ship about 1500 years ago.

What power moves this ship?

How is it steered?

Saxon ships

Remains of Roman ships have been found by archaeologists. So too have boats which belonged to the Saxon settlers who came to Britain after the Romans. The most famous of these in Britain is at Sutton Hoo in Suffolk, where the *impression* of a great open rowing boat was found under a mound of earth. It was about 27m long and 4.25m at its widest point. There was no place to put a mast and it was probably steered by a large paddle at the stern.

This is a picture of the site. All the wood of the boat has rotted away and left behind just the mark or impression of the planks and nails. Archaeologists think it was rowed by 40 men. How might they have worked this out?

This is a modern artist's idea of what it looked like.

36

Viking ships

Over 1100 years ago the Vikings began to invade Britain from Denmark, Norway and Sweden, arriving in their warships called longboats. This one was found in Norway, buried under a mound of earth like the boat at Sutton Hoo.

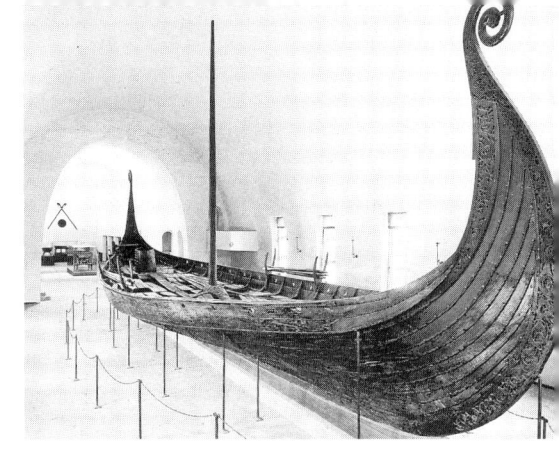

Here is an article from a newspaper about a rudder which was washed up on a beach in East Anglia not very long ago.

Viking rudder 'rare and exciting find'

MARITIME experts have described an ancient ship's rudder washed up on Southwold beach as "a rare and exciting find".

The rudder, 14 feet long and extremely well preserved, is the second to be found at Southwold.

The relic, technically known as a side rudder, would have been used to steer a mighty Viking ship, and is estimated to be about 1,000 years old, probably dating from 900 to 1100 AD.

It had lain hidden and protected beneath the seabed—hence its superb condition—until heavy seas disturbed its resting place and washed it up at Easton Broad, just north of Southwold, a week ago.

It was found by a Southwold boat builder and fisherman, Mr. Nobby Hutton, of Fairfield.

It will go to the maritime museum to be preserved and hopefully put on display.

• The Viking side rudder washed up at Southwold.

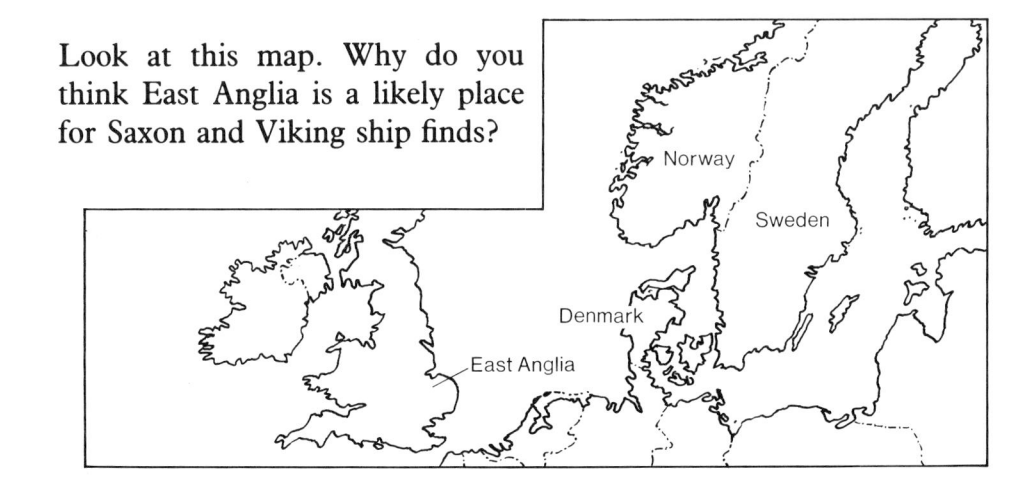

Look at this map. Why do you think East Anglia is a likely place for Saxon and Viking ship finds?

The middle ages

Ships of medieval times were in many ways similar to the ships of the Vikings or Norsemen.

The town seals of coastal towns like a) Winchelsea, b) Rye and c) Ipswich often show ships and they can tell us quite a lot about ship design.

Look carefully at the ships. The part of the vessel at the bow is called a *forecastle*. This is where the crew and stores were kept. The other end of the vessel is called the *aftercastle*.

Can you see what the sailors used to steer ships a) and c)?

Notice how many masts each of these ships has. Trade was growing and people needed bigger ships that could carry more cargo more quickly. More speed meant more sails and more sails meant more masts. By the end of the middle ages, about 500 years ago, 3-masted sailing ships were common.

a)

b)

c)

Tudor sailors

Improvements in steering, improved methods of using the wind, and better ways of navigating led to the building of bigger ships. Longer ocean voyages of exploration and discovery became possible. This was the time of Francis Drake and Walter Raleigh.

You have probably heard of the Mary Rose, a famous Tudor ship which sank in 1545. She has now been raised from the sea. This is what she looks like now and what she looked like originally. Historians have been able to find out a great deal about Tudor ships from the Mary Rose.

The Mary Rose had been buried on the seabed for 437 years. The silt (a mixture of mud and clay) had preserved the timbers.

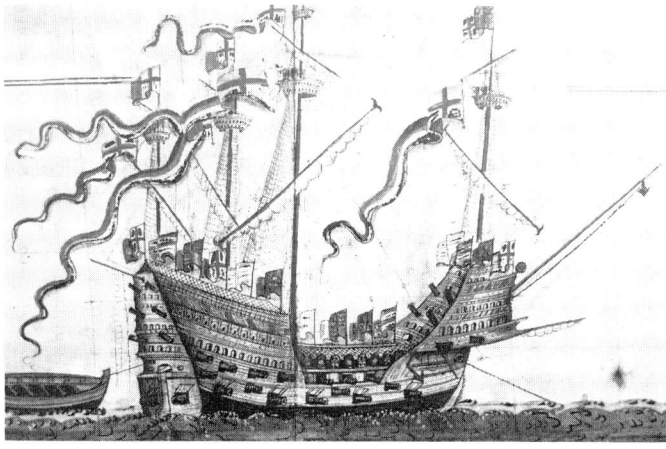

What differences can you see between the Mary Rose and the ships on the town seals?

What has happened to the castles?

Have the sails and the masts changed?

The clippers

Sea journeys used to take a long time in the days when the wind and sails were the only power. Some cargoes spoil if they are kept too long. Fresh meat, for example, could not be carried.

Ship-builders designed sailing ships which would go very fast, though still not fast enough to bring back meat from Australia or New Zealand. The clippers were famous sailing ships built to bring tea back from China and India. Often it was a race. The first ship back would get the best price for the tea.

This painting shows the famous race in 1866 between the clippers Taeping and Ariel. It began 16 000 miles away from Britain in China. The picture shows them in the English Channel at the end of the race. Taeping won by twenty minutes. What other type of ship can you see in this picture?

Voyages were quicker than they had been, but often uncomfortable, as the diary of John Rorke, aboard the clipper *Loch Vennachar* in 1877, shows.

> Thursday April 12th 1877 Rose at 7.45 a.m. Sea very rough, a little rain. We will soon be off the Bay of Biscay. After turning into bed last night it began to get very rough. About 2 a.m. this morning I awoke with the noise of the seas washing right over the deck house. This ship was rolling very much, so much so that it was hardly impossible to keep in bed, every moment I expected to be thrown out. She had too much sail on con:

What changes can you see between the shape of tea clippers and the Mary Rose? Why do you think the clippers have so many sails?

Steam boats

People experimented with steam engines. Steam engines were used to pull trains and could be used in ships. Look at this picture of the paddle-steamer Britannia, which began a transatlantic service in 1840. It has paddles at the sides and no propeller, or screw.

Why do you think the paddle steamer has sails?

What advantages did steam ships have over sailing ships?

In 1845 propellers were proved to be better than paddle wheels when the propeller-driven Rattler and the paddle-steamer Alecto had a tug-of-war. The Rattler towed the Alecto backwards.

Ships had always been made of wood, but it was not strong enough for steam-driven boats. So iron ships were made.

You may be able to visit the Great Britain in Bristol. It was built in 1843 and was the first really successful large steamship with a propeller.

Iron ships could be much bigger than wooden ones, and they needed to be in order to carry the large amounts of coal needed for the steam engines. Gradually engineers found out how to make smaller engines which did not use so much coal. Now we use oil for our big ships and some are enormous.

What sort of ships are these?

Why do you think they are so huge?

Can you find any similarities between these ships and the others you have looked at in this chapter?

A table of sources

Look at pictures A to H. They show ships from the periods of history mentioned in this chapter.

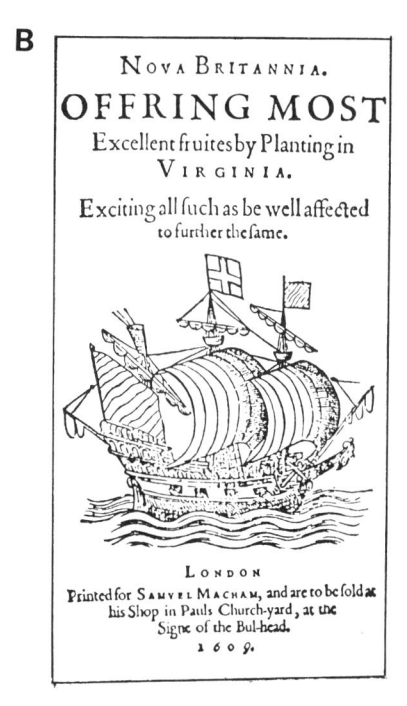

A

B

C

CONTAINERS THROUGH THE PORT OF LIVERPOOL

D

E

F

G

H

43

Copy the table. Look carefully at pictures A–H and try to put them in chronological order, the oldest first.

Put the ship's letter in the first column. In the second column put the kind of ship shown.

Think about what sort of evidence is being used. Is it a photograph, part of a manuscript or perhaps an advert? Write your answer in the column headed 'Source'.

In the last column try to fill in the major differences between each ship and the one which comes before it. Leave the top box empty and work downwards.

Ship	Type of Ship	Source	Differences

Bus, tram and trolley

Public transport

If you do not use a car perhaps you share a bus or train with other members of the public. This is why we call buses and trains "public transport". Before private cars were common, people used public transport a lot more. Buses are still common in our towns and cities, but people use them less.

Here is a table showing the number of passenger journeys made in years since 1951. Because it would take a lot of space and time to write out huge numbers in a long list, the last six noughts are often left out. So 16 623 means 16 623 millions and 6185 means 6185 millions. It is important to explain that this has been done, so 'millions' has been put at the top of the column to make everything clear.

We have made a graph from the table.

Year	Passenger Journeys (millions)
1951	16 623
1955	15 887
1959	13 938
1963	12 732
1967	10 617
1971	8639
1975	8168
1979	7100
1983	6210
1985	6177

CSO, Annual Abstract of Statistics

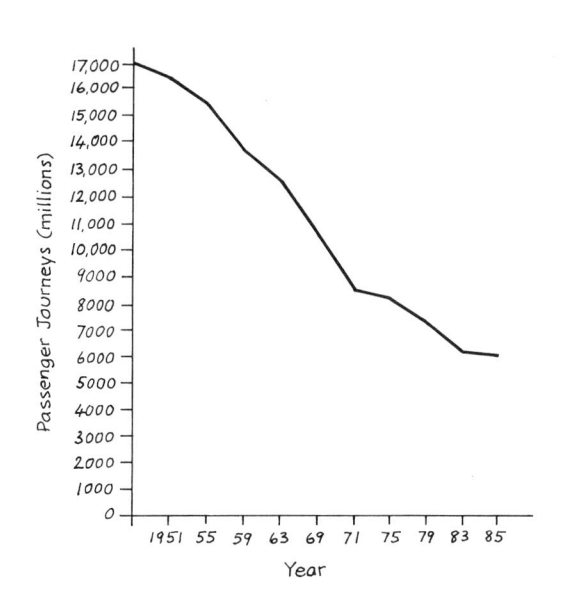

1. What would you expect to happen to the number of passenger journeys in the near future?
2. Make a list of reasons which you think might explain why the number of passenger journeys gets smaller.

Trends

Not many years ago public road transport was often a family's only way of getting about — going shopping, going to work or going to school. As time has passed, there have been changes. When we expect a change to continue into the future, we call it a *trend*. What trends can you see in this table?

Number of Vehicles

Year	Single-decker coaches	Double-decker buses	Total Buses	Trolleys	Tramcars
1951	41 393	33 687	75 080	3985	3531
1955	38 926	35 646	74 572	3716	2143
1959	36 183	37 376	73 559	2862	672
1963	36 518	39 820	76 338	1143	111
1967	37 190	37 095	74 285	254	108
1971	41 613	31 061	72 674	16	89
1975	48 022	28 775	76 797		101
1979	47 015	25 835	72 850		92
1983	44 786	25 326	70 112		79
1985	42 875	24 923	67 798		79

CSO, Annual Abstract of Statistics

Make a graph for the trolleys and tramcars and a similar one for the total number of buses.

1. What has happened to the number of trolleybuses and tramcars since 1951?
2. Why are no figures recorded for trolleybuses after 1971?
3. Why do you think that the number of single-decker coaches has gone up while the number of double-decker buses has gone down?
4. As public transport has become less popular, how do people travel?

Statistics

Information shown in graphs and tables of figures is known as *statistics*. Great Britain, like many other countries, keeps statistics about all its road-users. By keeping such a record we hope to spot trends. For example, if we can see from the statistics that more and more people are travelling in their own cars, we know that we must plan better roads and car parks.

The statistics we have given in this section so far have all come from a book called the *Annual Abstract of Statistics*. You can find these in your local Reference Library.

Timetables

Not all tables of figures are statistical tables. Here are tables which you might be more familiar with — timetables.

The information in this table is taken from timetables for the Ipswich Borough Transport Number 8 Bus and Trolleybus Service.

Service No 8 from Ipswich–Cornhill		from Tower Ramparts Bus Stn.
1927 To Bramford Rd.	1939 To Bramford Rd.	1986 To Maypole
6.56 a.m.	6.51 a.m.	6.20 a.m.
7.00 a.m.	then every 5 minutes until	then every 20 minutes until
7.10 a.m.	7.01 p.m.	7.20 a.m.
7.26 a.m.	7.07 p.m.	then every 10 minutes until
then every 10 minutes until	7.13 p.m.	6.00 p.m.
10.36 p.m.	7.22 p.m.	6.25 p.m.
10.53 p.m.	7.25 p.m.	then every 30 minutes until
11.03 p.m.		10.25 p.m.
		11.00 p.m.

1. Which years does it cover?
2. Work out how many buses ran each day. This may take you some time, but it is real historical detective work.
3. Why do you think buses were more frequent in the past? (If you are not sure, look back at David's surveys on p. 4 which found that many different forms of transport are now used.)

Here are the number 8's routes for 1927 and 1986:
  1927 Cornhill, Westgate St., St Matthews St., Norwich Road, Bramford Rd., Adair Rd.

1986 Tower Ramparts Bus Station, St Matthews St., Norwich Rd., Bramford Rd., Adair Rd., Henniker Rd., Bennet Rd., Bramford Lane, Ulster Avenue, Lovetofts Drive, Whitehouse Rd., Goddard Rd., Bury Rd., Old Norwich Rd., Maypole.

Why do you think there is such a difference? Do you think the places in the 1986 route existed in 1927?

The number 8 has always been a single-decker bus. This picture explains why.

Public transport in your area

Not long ago most people used buses, trams and trolleybuses because they did not have cars. The best way to find out what public transport was like in your area is to ask questions. Lots of people will remember what the buses or trams were like in the past. Perhaps your parents or grandparents will help you by answering your questions.

It is a good idea to plan the questions to ask. First of all, look at some books about buses, trams or trolleys. If you can't find any, the pictures on page 49 will help. You can find out where they came from by looking at the acknowledgements on the inside back cover.

Copy the table. Look carefully at pictures A–G and pick out the tram and trolleybus. How are trams and trolleybuses different from buses?

Try to put the buses into chronological order, the oldest first. Put the letter of the bus in the left hand column and in the second column write down one difference between it and the one which comes before it. Leave the top box empty and work downwards.

Bus	Differences

Conducting an interview

Write down some questions which you think might help you in your interview with someone who remembers using public transport in the past. It might help you to show them pictures like those in this section.

Decide how you are going to record their replies. A tape-recorder might be useful.

Do not be afraid of not following your question-sheet if you have a talkative aunt or grandparent. Stories are much more fun than short answers.

If you interview several people, make a little booklet called perhaps 'Memories of the Buses'.

Here is part of a question-sheet which might help you with yours.

> Can you remember going on a bus when you were small?
>
> How much did it cost?
>
> What were the buses like?
>
> What was it like riding on the buses in the rush hour? In the snow and fog?
>
> What changes have you noticed about travel on the buses?

And here is part of an interview which some children made.

> Rachel: What were buses like?
>
> Grandma: They were horse-drawn at first. Then the trams came next. The first tram came down the Mile End Road full of lights, and for a treat my Mother took me up to the corner where it came along. We were so frightened and buried ourselves against the wall when we saw this huge vehicle coming along all lit up with no horses dragging it, and we wondered whether it would come off the road and run into us. But it was quite an excitement because it was the first tram.

Have you read *In My Time*? If you have, you will know that memories are not always reliable. How and where could you check the facts mentioned in the interviews? The historical value of people's memories is further discussed in *Thanks for the Memory*.

Motor cars

The life and death of a family car

Not very long ago cars were too expensive for the ordinary family. Henry Ford, an American, produced the first cheap car in 1908, though it was a good many years before ordinary families in Great Britain could afford a car. Henry Ford also mass-produced his cars on a moving assembly line, which is how the family car has been made ever since.

Your car began its life like this on a factory production line.

It will probably end its life like this in a scrapyard.

A lot happens to a car between production line and scrapyard.

Car documents

Many of the things which happen are recorded on papers such as bills, receipts, certificates and forms. You probably have some of these at home because some of the documents are very important. From them you might be able to work out events in your car's history.

Here is a collection of documents about my cars. If you were a historian who discovered them many years later, you would be able to find out a lot from these pieces of paper.

First of all find the documents which a driver must have by law. Then try answering these questions.
1. How many cars can you find evidence of?
2. How many different addresses do the documents show that this driver has had? Put a date against each one if you can.
3. Describe the Allegro. Who was the previous owner?
4. What repair work was done to the Allegro? What sort of shop is Kwik Fit? What other motorists' shops can you think of?
5. Which documents show that a vehicle was in a roadworthy condition?
6. Describe OUB 878P. What sort of things happened to it?
7. Find the driving licence. How is this different from a modern driving licence?
8. How might the information on the Vehicle Registration Document be used?

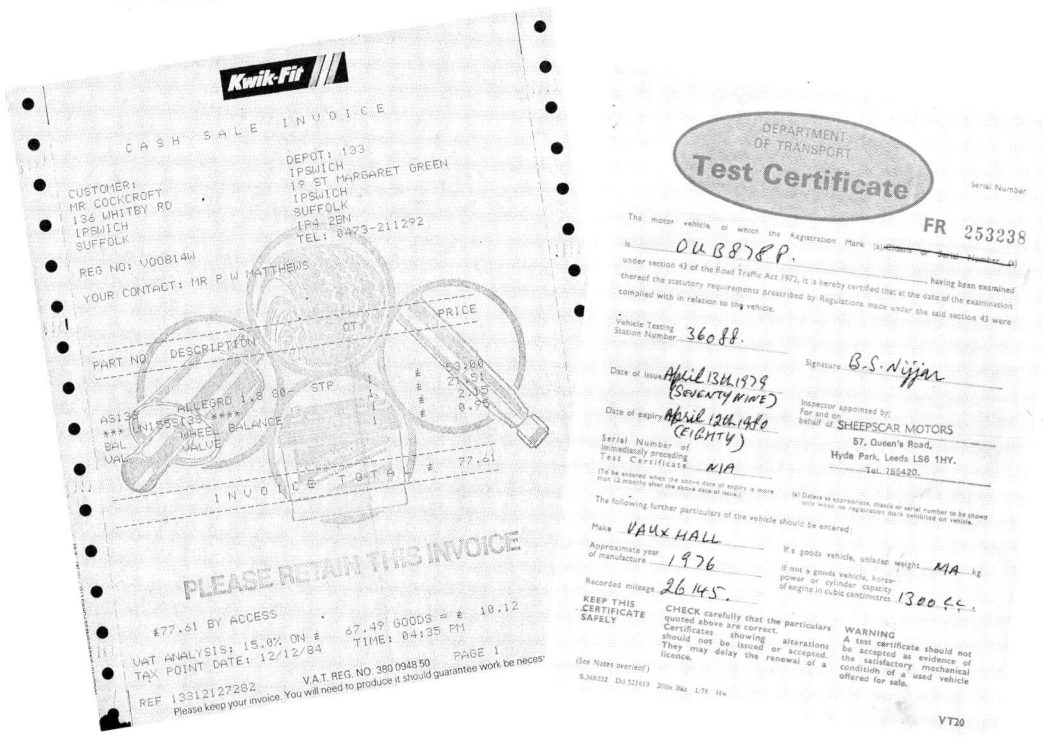

Tax Disc

90545400
EXPIRES
30:9:85

VOO 814W
AUSTIN
6 months £55

BRUNSWICK RD
28 MR 85

VT29 — Check List for Vehicle Inspection

Department of Transport — CUSTOMER'S COPY (Revised June 1983)

Vehicle Reg. No. or Chassis No: VOO 814W Make & Model: Allegro 1.3 Approx. year of manufacture: 1980 Recorded mileage: 37,372

Code	Testable Item	Testers Manual Reference	Pass	Fail	Remarks
01	**Section I – Lighting Equipment**				
02	Oblig. Front Lamps	I/1	✓		
03	Oblig. Rear Lamps	I/1	✓		
04	Oblig. Headlamps	I/2	✓		
05	Headlamp Aim	I/6	✓		
06	Stop Lamps	I/3	✓		
07	Rear Reflectors	I/4	✓		
08	Direction Indicators	I/5	✓		
09					
10	**Section II – Steering & Suspension**				
11	Steering Controls	II/1		X	Pulls to N.S. Repaired
12	Steering Mechanism	II/3		X	K Bal
13	Power Steering		NA		
14	Transmission Shafts	II/2,2.19,III/4,4	✓		
15	Stub Axle Assemblies	II/5	✓		
16	Wheel Bearings	II/4	✓		
17	Suspension	II/5,6,7,8,9	✓		
18	Shock Absorbers	II/10	✓		
19					
20	**Section III – Braking System**				
21	Service Brake Condition	III/3,4	✓		
22	Parking Brake Condition	III/1,2	✓		
23	Service Brake Efficiency	III/5,6,7,8	✓		
24	Parking Brake Efficiency	III/5,6,7,8	✓		
25	Service Brake Balance	III/5,6,7,8	✓		
26					
27	**Section IV – Tyres & Wheels**				
28	Tyre Type	IV/1	✓		
29	Tyre Condition	IV/1	✓		
30	Roadwheels	IV/2	✓		
31					
32	**Section V – Seat Belts**				
33	Security of Mountings	V/1	✓		
34	Condition of Belts	V/1	✓		
35	Operation	V/1	✓		
36					
37	**Section VI – General Items**				
38	Windscreen Washers	VI/2	✓		
39	Windscreen Wipers	VI/2	✓		
40	Horn	VI/4	✓		
41	Condition of Exhaust System	VI/3	✓		
42	Effectiveness of Silencer	VI/3	✓		
43	Condition of Vehicle Structure	VI/5	✓		

During the test on this vehicle the defects mentioned below were noticed, which in the opinion of the tester, render the vehicle DANGEROUS for use on the road.

Warning: A person who drives a dangerously defective vehicle on the road is liable to prosecution and the insurance may not be operative.

Note: The MOT Testers Manual is a comprehensive guide to the inspection procedures applied during the MOT test. It sets out in detail the statutory requirements that vehicles have to meet, methods of inspection and the prescribed manner may be purchased through...

Pass Cert No: 5808774419 (VT20)

Invoice — Leeds Autocars

VAUXHALL/BEDFORD Main Dealer
Leeds Autocars sales & service Limited
Roseville Road, Leeds LS8 5DT
Telephone 0532-41551

VAT Registration No. 169 2554 37

Mr. J.C. Cockcroft,
590 Scott Hall Road,
LEEDS.

№ 24980 /LD
Tax Point: 21st September, 1977

To one used 1976 Vauxhall Viva 2 door in colour Champagne. Sold as seen, tried and approved, and sold with a Superline warranty – number 12/VX/14342.

£1625.00

Less deposit of £25.00.

Reg. no: OUB 878P   Stock no: 6893
Chassis no: 9011D FX 102027   Date first reg: 8.4.76
Engine no: 1644650   Mileage:

Input tax deduction has not been and will not be claimed by us in respect of the car sold on this invoice.

I/We have purchased the aforementioned vehicle, reg. no: OUB 878P for the sum of £1625.00.

Signed..............
Date..............

Norwich Union Insurance Letter

Norwich Union Fire Insurance Society Limited
Scottish Union and National Insurance Company
Norwich Union Chambers, 20 Princes Street, Ipswich IP1 1RD
Telephone 0473 213721

Manager: B C Henderson ACII

Date: 5.3.81
Telephone extension: 32
Our reference: C/C/7937NB37188/0

J. COCKCROFT ESQ
136. WHITBY ROAD
IPSWICH
IP4 LRG

Your reference: (IT IS ESSENTIAL THAT OUR REFERENCE BE QUOTED IN ANY REPLY)

WITHOUT PREJUDICE

Accident Date: 5.

Dear Sir/Madam,

Our Insured: R. RACE
Your Insured/Client/Vehicle: OUB 878P

Please refer to the box/es ticked below. Where a reply is requested please do so as quickly as possible.

1. ☐ The claim is being investigated and we are therefore not yet able to comment on liability.
2. ☐ We have not received a report of this accident and are contacting our Insured.
3. ☐ We have your letter dated _____. Please explain in FULL why you are holding our Insured and give details of all independent evidence which you have.
4. ☐ We have no objection to repairs being carried out at £81.00 plus any parts shown makers list price. At this stage we cannot undertake to pay for repairs.
5. ☑ Forward the estimate/account/documentary evidence of the outlay you wish us to consider.
6. ☐ Our Engineer wishes to inspect the vehicle. Where and when can it be inspected during normal Engineer will make contact.
7. ☐ We are unable to accept that our Insured was at fault and thus we cannot deal with your claim.
8. ☐ The vehicle is considered beyond economical repair. Pre-accident and salvage values are respectively. The salvage should be disposed of immediately.
9. ☐ Without admission of liability we are prepared to offer/enclose cheque for £
10. ☐ The circumstances of the accident show that our Insured was blameless. We therefore our outlay. Details are enclosed/will follow. Please let us have your cheque for £ letter to your Insurers. For their information our cover is Comprehensive/T.P. Excess £ by return of post.
11. ☐ Please reply to our letter dated _____.
12. ☐ If we do not hear from you within the next 14 days we shall instruct Solicitors to...
13. ☑ Please provide the name and address of the vehicle insurers and the relevant policy...
14. ☑ Are you/your clients registered for V.A.T.?
15. ☐

Yours faithfully,

A. Buckmore
for Branch Manager

Norwich Union Fire Insurance Society Limited. Registered in England no 99122. Registered Office Surrey Street Norwich.
Scottish Union and National Insurance Company (a company limited by shares). Registered in Scotland no 211.

MC 208 - 750 - 5.80 (THIRD PARTY)

USED CAR INVOICE

CUSTOMER'S COPY   **UC 00078**

Sold by: Telephone 622173 and 624329
E. C. FRANKLAND LTD
VAUXHALL & BEDFORD RETAIL DEALERS
Bayswater Garages
7, Arundel Terrace and 20, Roseville Road, Leeds LS8 5DS
Registered in London No. 859914   V.A.T. No 169 5481 35

Invoice No / Date of Transaction: 3.8.74
Number: 72
Stock Book / Day Book Folio (if any):

Sold to: John Charles Cockcroft (Name)
11 Lindsworth Court
Marshall Hall Rd, Kings Norton, Birmingham (Address)

Particulars of car –
1. Make: Vauxhall
2. Model or Type: Viva HC
3. Registration No: UUG436H
4. Engine No (if any): 1311346
5. Chassis No: 97331 HE 331446
6. Month and year car first registered in UK: 1st Nov 1969
7. The Milometer reading is: 42852
8. The approximate true mileage, if different from the milometer reading:

Declaration by the buyer (except where the sale is made to a finance company in which case it must be made by the person acquiring the car from the finance company under a hire purchase or conditional sale agreement) –
I declare that I am the buyer of the car described above at the price stated below.
or
(where the car is sold to a finance company)
I acknowledge receiving delivery of the car described above.

Date: 3.8.74   Signature: John C. Cockcroft

Declaration by the seller –
Input tax deduction has not been and will not be claimed by me in respect of the car sold on this invoice.

Date: 3.8.74   Signature: B Frankland

E. C. FRANKLAND LTD. PRICE   £ 425.00
LICENCE
                              £ 425.00

Receipt

161   Date: 2.8.74
Received of £425.00
Mr J.C.Cockcroft
the sum of four hundred and twenty five pounds only Cheque
For S B Frankland Ltd

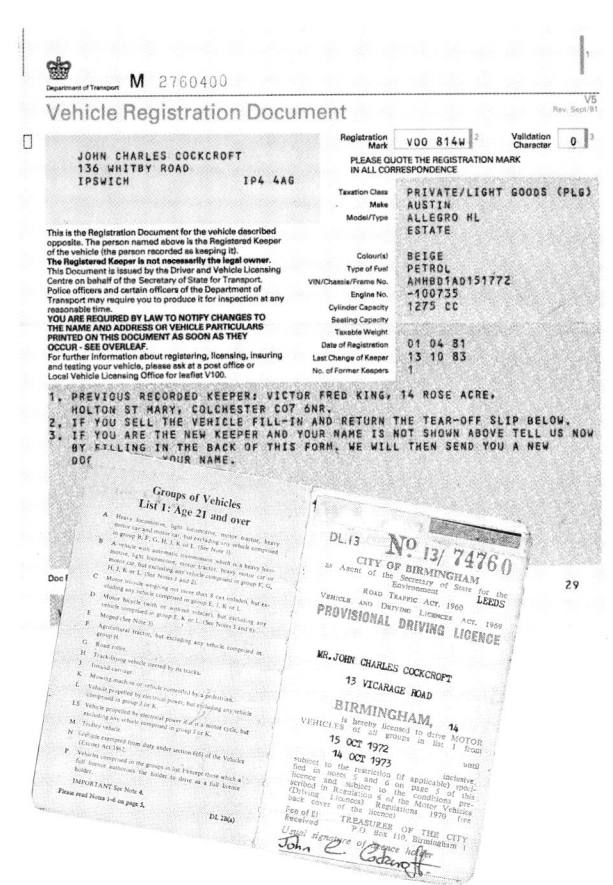

Changes in family cars

Most families change their car from time to time. Sometimes families have more than one car. Perhaps your parents or grandparents can remember several different cars they have had. Ask them what differences they noticed between their cars. What changes have they noticed in the roads, traffic rules and services on the roads? Ask them if they have photographs of their cars. Cars often appear in photographs though they may not be the main feature.

Here are the two cars mentioned in the documents on pages 52–54. Why were they photographed, do you think?

Find as many photographs of cars as you can. Bring some from home if possible. Arrange them into chronological (date) order. If you cannot find enough, here are some which show the changes that have been made in the family car since it began.

A

Model 'T' Ford   1910s

B

Ford 8 h.p. Model 'Y'   1930s

C

Morris Minor   Late 1940s/50s

D

Vauxhall Cresta   1950s

E

Mini   1960s

F

Ford Escort   1980s

Copy the table. Look at pictures A–F carefully and think about how cars have changed to become more comfortable, safer, stronger, more stream-lined.

Try to fill in the differences between each car and the one which comes before it in the column headed 'Differences'. Leave the top box empty and work downwards.

Car	Differences
A	
B	
C	
D	
E	
F	

Past and future

How do you think cars will change in the future? How will the shape alter? How will the insides of cars change? What instruments will cars have that they do not have now? Design a car of the future. Label the important features.

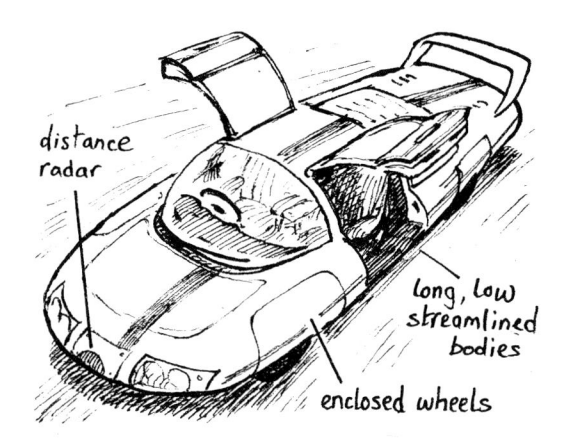

Imagine you are going on a long car journey — say from London to Edinburgh. Look up these cities in an atlas to see now far apart they are. How would you prepare your car for the trip? What might it need on the way? Would you have to make stops on the way? What for?

Imagine you made the same journey in 1913 in the Model 'T' Ford. How would your preparations be different? What difficulties might you expect to meet on the journey? Would the journey be as comfortable? What stops would you need to make? Would you get there as quickly as in the modern car?

Number plates

All vehicles are *registered* and have *registration plates* on them.

Registration plates are often a good guide to where a car comes from because all *licensing authorities* are given letters which only they use. The letters I and Z, for example, only appear in Irish registrations, and the letter S generally in Scottish registrations. You can find a list of letters and places in an Automobile Association (AA) leaflet called *Vehicle Index Marks in the British Isles*. Here is the A section, for example. There is no room for us to print the whole list, so ask your teachers or parents if they have an AA leaflet which you can look at.

AA	Bournemouth	**AJ**	Middlesbrough	**AS**	Inverness
AB	Worcester	**AK**	Sheffield	**AT**	Hull
AC	Coventry	**AL**	Nottingham	**AU**	Nottingham
AD	Gloucester	**AM**	Swindon	**AV**	Peterborough
AE	Bristol	**AN**	Reading	**AW**	Shrewsbury
AF	Truro	**AO**	Carlisle	**AX**	Cardiff
AG	Hull	**AP**	Brighton	**AY**	Leicester
AH	Norwich	**AR**	Chelmsford		

Look at the cars in the teachers' car park. Find out from the number plates where the cars began their life on the road. If they do not belong in your area ask the teacher-owners if they know why.

On a modern number plate there is always a letter by itself. This tells you when the car was first registered and is a good clue as to how old the car is. Make a list of the letters which mean a particular date, like this:

> D 1986/7
> C 1985/6
> B 1984/5
> A 1983/4
> Y 1982/3

and so on. The letters I, O, Q and Z are never used to show the date in a registration letter because they can too easily be read as numbers.

Look again at your car numbers from the teachers' car park. Who has the newest car? The oldest?

For example: VOO 814W means that a car was first registered in Essex (OO) between 1980-1981(W).

Sometimes cars have number plates that are different from those that you usually see. These might be foreign cars. You may be able to see where they come from by the international registration letters attached to the back of the car. For example, GB means a car from Great Britain. Where do these vehicles come from? Use the AA leaflet again to help you.

Make a map of Europe and inside each country put its international registration letters.

Car trends in Britain

The approximate numbers of cars in Britain since 1930 are as follows:

    1930   1 million
    1940   1½ million
    1950   2½ million
    1960   5½ million
    1970   11 million
    1980   16 million

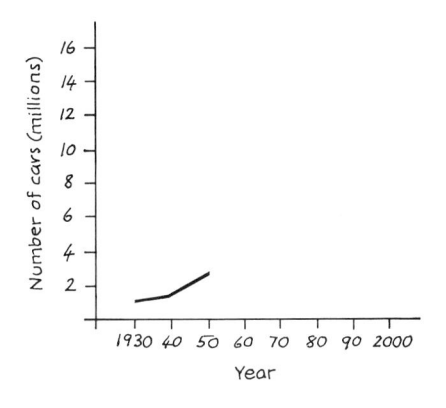

Use these figures to complete this graph. Notice the trend.

How many cars do you think there might be in the year 2000?

The increase in the number of cars has led to a great improvement in the road network and to the opening of the motorway system in the late 1950s. Motorways with their three lanes and comparatively straight routes allow motor vehicles, which carry goods as well as people, to travel at high speeds.

Make a list of the advantages and disadvantages of the motorway system.

Copy this map of Britain showing the routes of the motorways. Find an up-to-date road map and name the motorways.

Why do you think the following major motorways were built: M1, M4, M5, M6, M8 and M25?

Transport in photographs

Comparing photographs

An easy way to see what transport was like in times gone by is to look at photographs. Almost any town scene will show some form of transport.

Look at the three photographs on these pages. They show the same street, called Briggate, in Leeds at different dates. Take each photograph in turn and make a list of all the different types of transport that you can see. Try to count the numbers of each type to estimate how important it was at that time.

What can you see in pictures A and B that you can't see in picture C? Why?

Notice how busy the street is in each photograph. In which photograph is the number of (1) pedestrians, (2) vehicles greatest?

A   *Briggate in the 1900s*

B   *Briggate in the 1930s*

Can you discover the time of day when each photograph was taken?

At what time of day would you expect the street to be a) busiest and b) quietest?

Street furniture

Most streets have things in them which we use in our day-to-day lives to help us. We need signposts, street lights, litter bins, pillar boxes, traffic lights, for example. We call these things *street furniture*.

Make three lists of the street furniture that you can see in each of the photographs. Put a cross next to any item to do with transport.

Which photograph has the most? Why do you think this is?

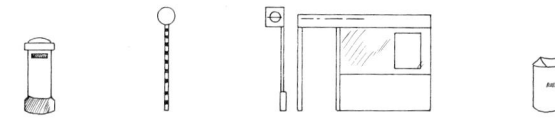

Do it yourself

If you want to find old photographs of your area, ask at your local library. Tell the librarians that you are especially interested in transport. They should be able to help you find old bus timetables, too.

C *Briggate today*

Change

Change sometimes happens because people want improvements. Trains, boats and planes are more comfortable, safer and faster than they used to be because people who use them want them to be better. Who would travel in a rickety car if they could find something better?

But improvements are not always improvements for everybody.

Imagine that a new motorway is built near your school. Here is a picture of the motorway with the opinions of some of the people who are affected by it. Can you think of any other people who would be affected and their opinions? Do you think the motorway should have been built?

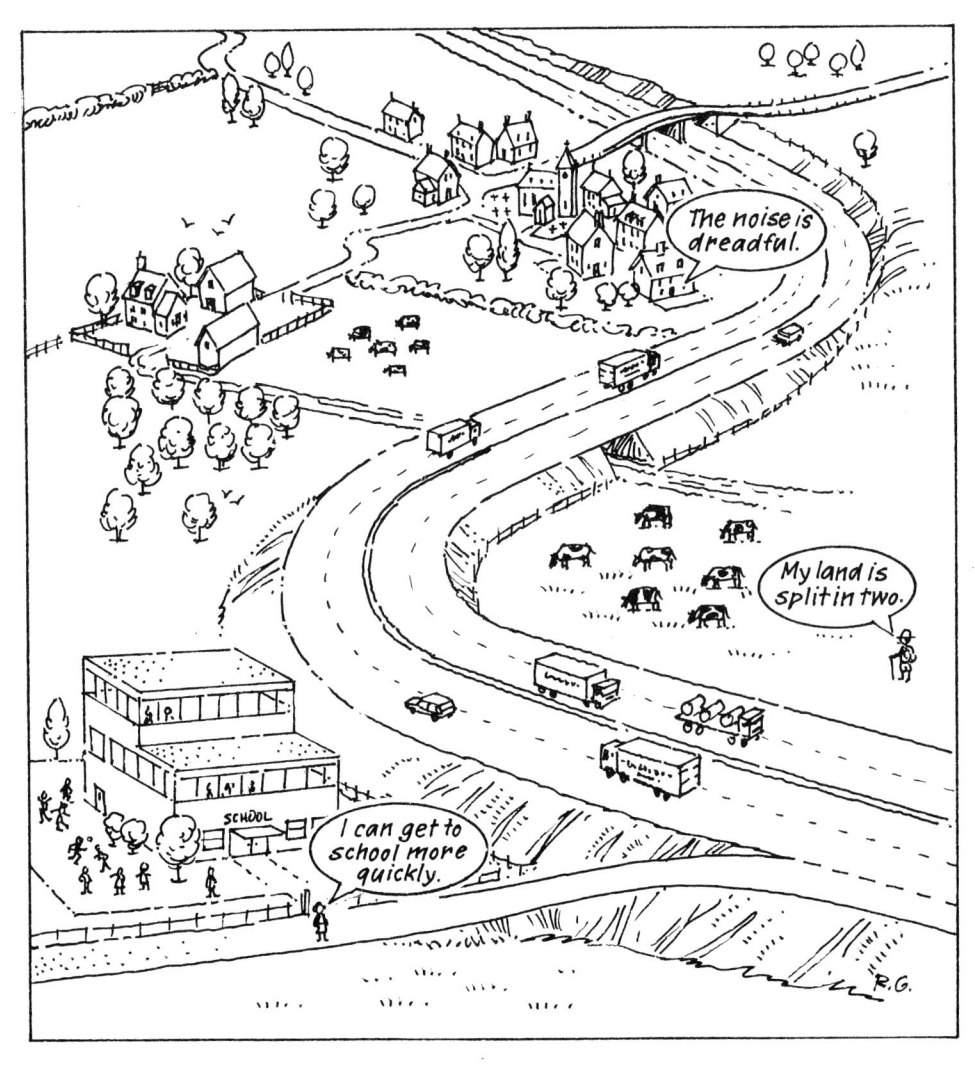

Flight

Long distances are usually measured in kilometres. Sometimes, however, people say that places are only 'minutes away'. They are talking of *time distance*.

How many minutes is your house away from a) your school, b) the centre of your town, c) London, d) Edinburgh, e) Cardiff, f) Belfast?

This shows Britain, the Atlantic Ocean and the USA. The scale-line shows the number of days taken to cross the Atlantic by clipper in the 1850s. The table shows the time taken by later forms of transport.

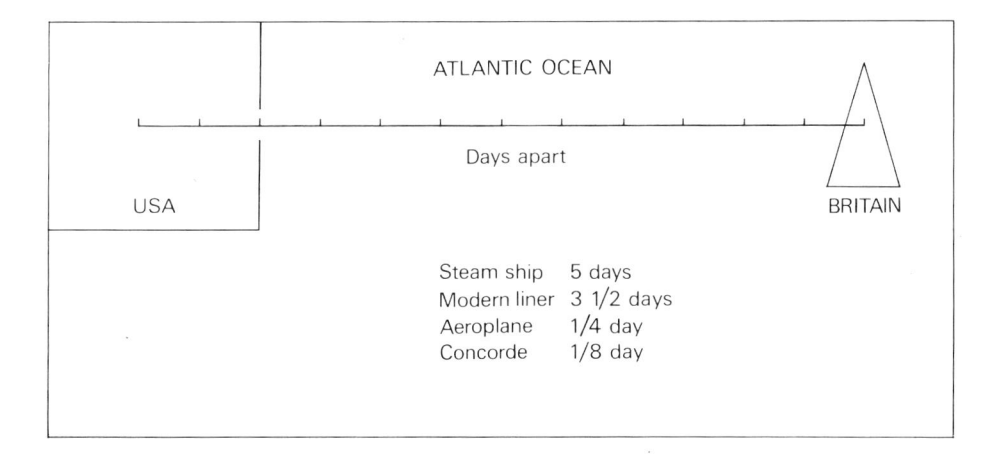

```
ATLANTIC OCEAN
            Days apart
USA                                           BRITAIN

        Steam ship      5 days
        Modern liner    3 1/2 days
        Aeroplane       1/4 day
        Concorde        1/8 day
```

1) Cut out a square to cover Britain. Label it Britain.
2) Put the piece of paper on the scale-line to show how many days it takes to cross the Atlantic by
   a) steam ship   b) modern liner   c) aeroplane   d) Concorde
3) What do people mean when they say that the world is 'shrinking'?

A smaller world is partly the result of air transport. Land and sea transport are often affected by barriers which they must avoid. Can you think of any? How might they be overcome? Air transport is better able to follow a direct route. But the early aeroplanes had their own difficulties. To find out more about them you will have to read *Flying through Time*, another book in the series.

INDEX

Act of Parliament 10, 11, 20
aqueduct 20
archaeologist 36

barges 24, 25
Beamish Open Air Museum 31
Bingley Five Rise Locks 21, 22
Briggate, Leeds 60, 61

clippers 39
coaches 32
coaching inns 13, 14
coracle 35
cutting 33, 34

Dickens, Charles 16
directories 19

embankment 33, 34

flange 27
Ford, Henry 51

Great White Horse Hotel, Ipswich 16

highwaymen 13

international registration letters 58
interview 48, 50

journeys 6, 7, 8, 14, 45, 57

Leeds and Liverpool Canal 19, 20
Liverpool and Manchester Railway 31, 32
locks 20–22
Locomotion 30, 31
long boats 37

Mary Rose 39
motorways 59
museums 26

National Railway Museum 28, 32, 33
navvies or navigators 21, 33

paddle steamers 41
plateways 26, 28
preserved railways 26
public transport 45–50

railway coaches 32
railway companies 28, 29, 34
railway tracks 26, 27
registration plates 57
roads 10, 11, 59
Rocket, the 32
Romans 35

Saltaire 22, 23
Saxons 36
Science Museum 32
Stage and mail coaches 13–18
statistics 4, 5, 45, 46, 59
steamboats 41, 42
Stephenson, George 28, 30
Stephenson, Robert 32
Stockton and Darlington Railway 28–31
street furniture 60
Surrey Iron Railway 28
Sutton Hoo 36
Swan with Two Necks, The 14, 15

time-distance 63
timetables 14, 15, 47
tollgates 17
tolls 10, 17, 22, 28
town seals 38
tunnels 20, 33, 34
Turnpike Trusts 10, 12

viaduct 33, 34
Vikings 37

wagonways 26